In the **Beginner Reader** level, **Step 4** builds on the sounds learned in previous steps and introduces new sounds and their letters:

e u r h b f ff l ll ss

AF729150

Special features:

Phonically decodable text builds reading confidence

Short sentences with simple language

Repetition of sounds in different words

Practice of words that cannot be sounded out

Summary page to reinforce learning

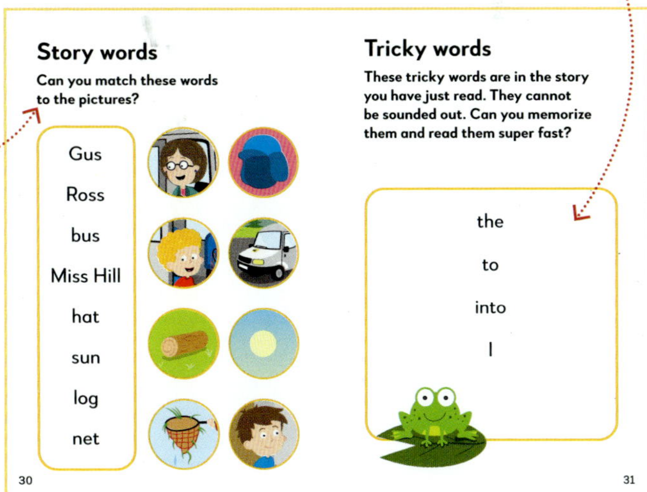

Ladybird

Phonics and Book Banding Consultant: Kate Ruttle

LADYBIRD BOOKS

UK | USA | Canada | Ireland | Australia
India | New Zealand | South Africa

Ladybird Books is part of the Penguin Random House group of companies whose addresses can be found at global.penguinrandomhouse.com.

www.penguin.co.uk www.puffin.co.uk www.ladybird.co.uk

Penguin Random House UK

Text adapted from *Huff! Puff! Run! – Ladybird I'm Ready for Phonics: Level 4*
first published by Ladybird Books 2014
Read It Yourself edition first published by Ladybird Books Ltd 2018
This edition published 2026
001

Printed in Dubai

The authorized representative in the EEA is Penguin Random House Ireland, Morrison Chambers, 32 Nassau Street, Dublin D02 YH68

A CIP catalogue record for this book is available from the British Library

ISBN: 978-0-241-74640-0

All correspondence to:
Ladybird Books
Penguin Random House Children's
One Embassy Gardens, 8 Viaduct Gardens, London SW11 7BW

MIX
Paper | Supporting responsible forestry
FSC® C018179
FSC www.fsc.org

Read It Yourself

The Fun Run

Written by Monica Hughes
Illustrated by Chris Jevons

Gus, Ross, Mum and Dad go to the fun run.

Gus has a lot of kit.

Ross has no kit and is fed up.

Miss Hill sets off the fun run. Mum and Dad tell Gus to run and run.

Ross is at the back.

Gus runs off but gets hot and has a nap.

Ross gets hot but runs on.

Ross gets back to Miss Hill.
Ross gets a medal.

Gus gets up.

Gus gets back and gets his medal.

Huff! Puff!

Story words

Can you match these words to the pictures?

Gus	Miss Hill
Ross	nap
fun run	medal

Tricky words

These tricky words are in the story you have just read. They cannot be sounded out. Can you memorize them and read them super fast?

to

the

go

I

no

Read It Yourself

Gus is Hot!

Written by Monica Hughes
Illustrated by Chris Jevons

Miss Hill, Gus and Ross
get on the bus.

Gus runs to the back of the bus.

Ross, Gus and Miss Hill
get off the bus.

Miss Hill tells Gus it is hot in the sun.

Ross and Gus sit on logs.
Ross dips his net into
the bog.

Gus rams his net into the bog.

Ross has a net. It is full of big bugs.

Gus tugs up his net,
and it is full of mud.

Back on the bus, Gus is ill.